Shape, Sculpt, and Roll

by Deborah Schecter

Contents

Scholastic Inc.

New York Toronto London Auckland Sydney Mexico City New De

Get ready to create with Crayola® Model Magic® Modeling Material!

Dear Young Artist,

Get ready for modeling fun! Funny-face Finger Puppets, a Friendly Froggy, and other great projects are waiting for you on the pages of this book. You're sure to come up with your own great ideas, too!

Dear Parent,

The projects in this book invite your child to explore the art of sculpting. Before trying them out, spend some time together experimenting with the modeling compound included in the kit. Squish it, roll it, mold it, and fold it! It's sure to spark lots of creative fun!

Deborah

Model Magic® Tips

1. Wet your fingertips if the Model Magic® starts to harden while you're working with it.

2. When you're finished with a project, let it dry overnight.

3. Seal leftover Model Magic® and unfinished projects in a plastic bag or plastic wrap. This will make them dry more slowly.

P.S. This book has lots of fun ideas for easy modeling projects that you can do. When you need more Model Magic® than you have in your kit, you can find it wherever Crayola® art materials are sold.

Mixing Colors

You can make lots of new colors using the five colors from your kit: red, blue, yellow, white, and green! Just knead together different colors of Model Magic® until they are blended. Here's how:

Red + Blue = Purple   Green + White = Light Green   Red + Yellow + Blue = Brown

Red + Yellow = Orange   Red + White = Pink

What happens when you mix two colors together halfway? You get this!

Modeling Tools

Here are a few ways you can use the tools in your kit. You're sure to come up with a lot more!

Cutters

Wheel Cutter

Plastic Knife

Now it's time for Model Magic® fun!

3-D ABCs

You can write your name with Crayola® Model Magic®!
It's easy to make the letters from A to Z!

1. Start by rolling pieces of Model Magic® into long and short logs. To make an "A," bend a long log into an arch. Your letters will stand up better if you make the bottoms a little fatter than the tops.

2. Use your fingers to press the pieces together. Then wet your fingertips with water and smooth away any cracks. Press down gently so that each letter can stand up by itself.

3. To make swirly letters twist together two different color logs.

4. Now decorate your letters!

 Polka Dots Roll little balls of Model Magic®. Press them onto your letters and then flatten them with your finger.

Stripes Roll thin strings. Press them side by side onto your letters.

Curly Shapes Roll thin strings to make swirly shapes, too! Curl them around and around your letter.

Tiny Triangles Flatten some Model Magic®. Then use your cutter to cut out triangle shapes. Press them onto your letters.

Now make your name. Create your own designs!

Cute Cutouts

Use your cutters to make adorable animals and other great shapes!

Rainbow Critters

1. Roll pieces of Model Magic® into thin ropes. Make ropes in lots of different colors.

2. Press the ropes together, side by side. Then flatten them with your hand.

3. Use an animal cutter from your kit to gently press out its shape.

4. Give your critter two eyes and a tail. To make eyes, roll two small white balls. Then make two smaller balls any color you want. Put together and press the eyes on your critter.

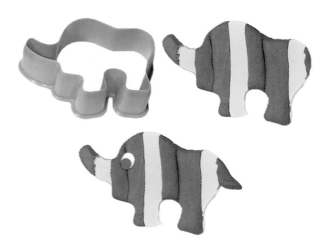

What other kinds of rainbow critters can you make?

Cutter Prints

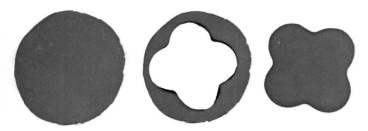 

1. Flatten a piece of Model Magic® with your hand. Press a cutter of your choice into the material. Then gently push out the shape.

2. Press your wheel cutter into the shape like this. Then lift it off.

fork

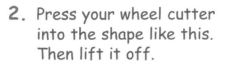

shell

3. Try making prints with buttons, shells, forks, and combs. What other things can you use to make prints?

Here's More!

- To make a pretty ornament, press a paper clip into the back of a shape before it dries.

- Poke a pencil through a shape before it dries. Then string it on a piece of yarn to wear!

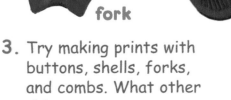

I'm Hungry! What's for Lunch?

It's time to make a yummy meal! (These foods may look good enough to eat, but remember they're just pretend.)

Pizza!

1. Make a ball of yellow Model Magic®. Then flatten it with your hand. Turn up the edges all around.

2. Add some red for tomato sauce. Then add bits of white for cheese.

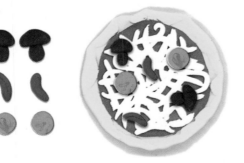

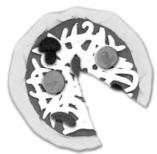

3. What else do you want on your pizza? Mushrooms? Peppers? Pepperoni?

4. Use your wheel cutter to take a slice!

A hamburger, a hot dog and french fries!

1. For a hamburger, flatten a little ball of brown Model Magic®.

1. Roll a hot dog using brown mixed with red.

1. To make french fries, roll a long thin piece of yellow. Using your plastic knife, cut french fry pieces.

2. Add lettuce with a thin piece of green. To add a tomato slice, flatten a ball of red.

2. Use yellow to shape a hot dog bun.

2. Make a plate for your french fries by flattening a piece of any color Model Magic®.

3. Then put all your hot dog pieces together! Want to add some mustard?

3. For hamburger buns, flatten two yellow balls a little bit. Now you can put your hamburger together!

3. Pile your french fries high on your plate!

What's for dessert? Turn the page to find out.

Sweet Shop!

Ice cream, cupcakes, cookies, candy—what's your favorite dessert?

Ice-cream Sundae

1. Roll some Model Magic® into a ball. Use your thumb to press a hole in the middle.

2. Pinch around the sides to make a dish. Add a base.

3. Knead together two different colors to make a swirly scoop of ice cream. Roll it into a ball. Then put the scoop in your dish.

4. Use brown to add drips of hot fudge. Spread the hot fudge over your ice cream.

5. How about some whipped cream? Roll long, thin strings of white. Curl them on top of the ice cream. Then add a cherry on top!

Tasty Cupcakes

1. Shape a piece of brown Model Magic® into a cupcake shape.

2. Flatten a ball of another color. Press it on top for icing.

3. Add a squiggle of frosting. Roll a long, stringy piece of white. Zigzag it on top of your cupcake.

Cookie Cutouts

1. Make little balls and flatten them. Use your cutters to cut out cookies. Then decorate them!

2. Make other kinds of cookies, too!

Swirly Candy Canes

1. Knead together some red and white Model Magic® until the colors are swirled.

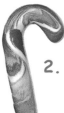

2. Roll the swirled colors into a long, thin log. Bend the top.

Add more sweets to your shop!

Let's Go to the Zoo!

Elephant Pencil Topper

This friendly elephant will always be ready to write with you!

1. What color do you want your elephant to be? Roll a fat ball of Model Magic®. This will be your elephant's head.

2. Roll two more balls and flatten them to add floppy ears!

3. Now flatten two small balls of white. Press them onto each ear.

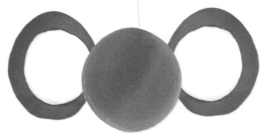

4. Press the ears onto your elephant's head.

5. For a trunk, roll a log. Use your plastic knife to make little lines on it. Then press the trunk onto the head and bend it up a little.

6. Time for the tusks! Make two thin logs of white. Add them on each side of the trunk. Bend up the ends a little bit.

7. Now for the eyes! Make them the same way you did for your Rainbow Critter on page 6.

8. Push your elephant's head onto the eraser end of a pencil.

Here's More! You can make other kinds of animal pencil toppers, too!

Balancing Beach Ball

Make a seal that does an amazing trick!

1. Make a fat log of Model Magic®. Mold it into a shape like this for the seal's body.

2. Now roll a ball for the head. Then mold a nose that points up.

3. Give your seal eyes, the same way you did for your Rainbow Critter on page 6.

4. Gently press the head onto your seal's body.

5. To add flippers, make two big and two small logs. Flatten them with your hand. Press them onto your seal's body. Let your seal dry.

6. While your seal is drying, make a beach ball for it to balance! Roll little balls of red, yellow, green, blue, and white Model Magic®. Squish them together and then roll the material into a ball.

What a terrific balancing act!

7. Use your plastic knife to poke a hole in the ball. Then press the ball gently onto your seal's nose.

Who's Hatching?

Peck, peck, peck . . . who's that pecking out of its shell?

1. Make two balls of white Model Magic®. Use your thumb to press a hole in the middle of each one.

2. Pinch around the sides with your fingers to make an eggshell shape.

3. Use your fingers to mold pointy shapes all around each half to look like broken shells.

4. Now make a baby chick. Make a round yellow body and a smaller yellow head. Press them together.

5. Add wings and feet.

6. Now for a beak! Flatten a small ball and make the ends pointy. Then fold it in half. Press it onto the head.

7. Give your chick eyes.

Time to hatch!
Let your chick
peck its way out!

8. Let your chick and
eggshells dry overnight.
Then put your chick
inside one of the shells.

Here's More!

You can make a baby dinosaur
hatching out of its egg, too!

Kangaroo Catch-All

Your kangaroo pal can hold lots of things for you.
Pennies, paper clips, marbles, and more!

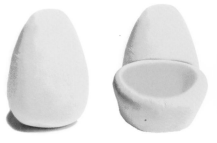

1. Roll a piece of Model Magic® into a ball. Use your thumb to press a hole in the middle.

2. Pinch around the sides with your fingers to make a bowl shape.

3. Make another shape that looks like this. Press it onto the bowl.

4. Roll some Model Magic® to make a head. Use your fingers to mold a long snout and pointy ears.

5. Give your kangaroo two eyes and a nose.

6. Gently press your kangaroo's head onto its body.

arms

 **legs**

7. Make arms and then legs with feet. Bend them as you see here. Then press them into place.

8. Roll a long pointy tail and press it onto the back of your kangaroo.

Now make a baby kangaroo to go in its mother's pouch! Or use your kangaroo to hold stuff!

Puppet Theater

Put on a play for your family with these finger-puppet friends!

Funny-face Finger Puppets

1. Flatten some Model Magic® into a rectangle.

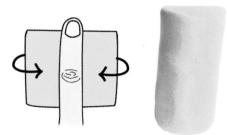

2. Wrap your flattened shape around your finger and press it together to make a sleeve. It should be loose enough to slip off your finger.

3. Roll a ball for a puppet head. Gently press it onto one end of the sleeve. Wet your fingertips to mold the two parts together.

4. Add two arms.

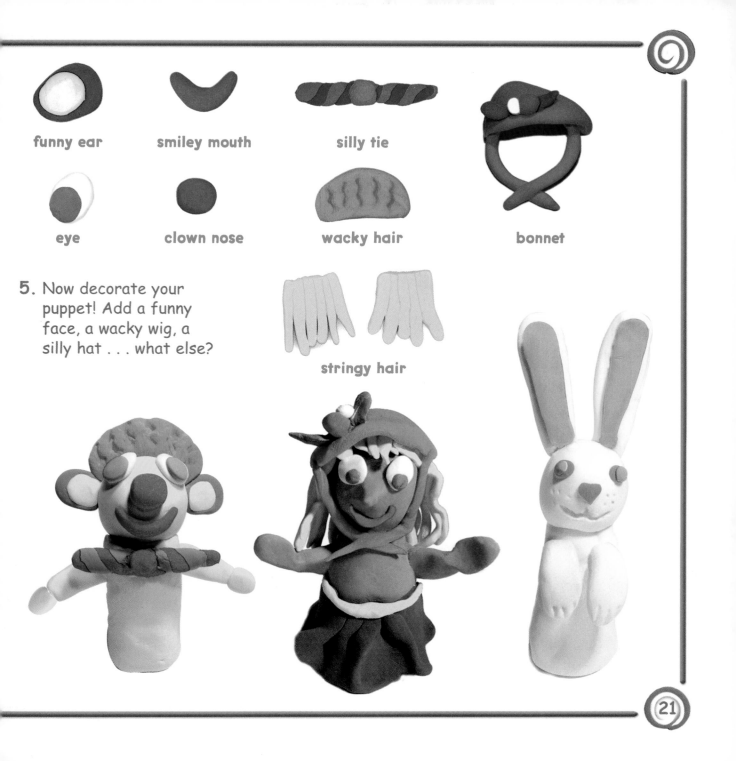

funny ear

smiley mouth

silly tie

bonnet

eye

clown nose

wacky hair

stringy hair

5. Now decorate your puppet! Add a funny face, a wacky wig, a silly hat . . . what else?

The Weather's Fine for Sailing

Get ready to set sail on your own little boat!

Sail Away, Sailboat!

1. Roll a thick log of Model Magic.® Use your thumb to press a hole in the middle.

2. Press more holes along the log.

3. Pinch the sides of the log all the way around to make a boat shape. Keep the sides thick.

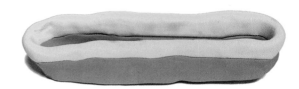

4. Use a different color of Model Magic® to roll a long string. Press it all around the top of your boat.

Here's More!

1. To make a sail, wrap a toothpick in some Model Magic®.

2. Flatten some Model Magic®. Use your plastic knife to cut out a triangle.

3. Press it onto the toothpick.

4. Put a lump of clay inside your boat to hold the toothpick sail in place. Then stick in your sail!

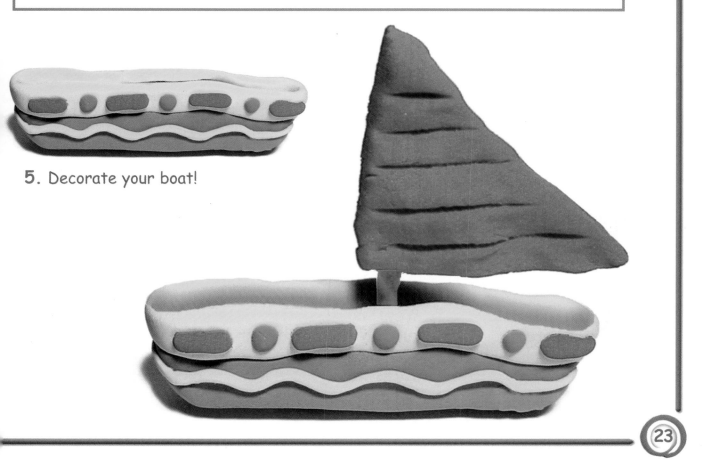

5. Decorate your boat!

Snappy Turtle

Snappy Turtle has come out of its shell to warm up in the sun!

1. Roll a ball of green Model Magic.® Then flatten it a little with your hand. This is your turtle's shell.

2. Use your plastic knife to make crisscross lines on the shell.

3. Use another color of Model Magic® and roll a small log for your turtle's head. Mold its mouth and its neck like this.

4. Make the turtle's eyes. Then press them onto its head.

5. Press the neck under the shell so that your turtle's head sticks out.

6. To make turtle toes, flatten small pieces of Model Magic.® Mold three toes on each foot. Then press the feet under your turtle's shell.

7. Add a pointy little tail!

8. Mold a rock for your turtle to sit on.

Who is Snappy Turtle looking at?
Turn the page to find out!

Friendly Froggy

Froggy's on the lookout for a lily pad to leap on. Ribbit! Ribbit!

1. What color will your froggy be? Roll two balls of Model Magic®, one big and one little.

2. Mold the little ball like this for your frog's head. Pinch the eyes with your fingers.

3. Make big froggy eyes. Then roll a string of pink for a mouth. Poke two dots for the nose with a pencil.

4. Press the head onto your frog's body.

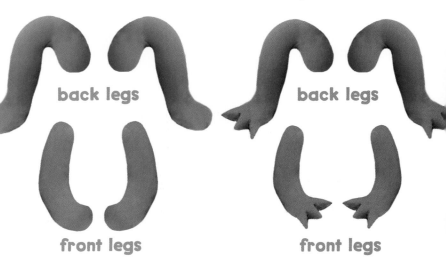

back legs

back legs

front legs

front legs

5. Roll four logs of Model Magic® for your frog's legs. Bend them like this.

6. Mold your frog's toes with your fingers.

Here's More!

Give your frog a lily pad to sit on!

1. Flatten a ball of green Model Magic®.

2. Use your plastic knife to cut out a triangle.

3. Add leafy lines with your plastic knife.

Then let your frog hop on!

7. Press your frog's legs onto its body.

Where do Snappy Turtle and Friendly Froggy live? Keep turning the pages to find out!

Crawly Creatures

Creep, crawl, flutter, fly. These critters get around in lots of different ways!

Little Ladybug

1. Flatten a ball of red Model Magic®. Use your plastic knife to make a line down the middle. Now your ladybug has wings.

2. How many spots does your ladybug have? Roll tiny balls of another color. Press them onto your ladybug's back.

3. To make a head, press a little oval onto your ladybug. For feelers, form little strings.

Dazzling Dragonfly

1. What color will your dragonfly be? Roll a long log for its body. Pinch one end to make it pointy.

2. Partly mix together two or three different colors of Model Magic®. Then form four skinny logs and flatten them to make wings.

3. Press two wings onto each side of your dragonfly. Add a little ball for a head and eyes.

Slithery Snail

1. Start with the snail's shell. Make two different color strings. One string can be made by swirling two colors.

2. Line up the strings and gently press them together. Then, starting at one end, roll them up.

3. Now start the snail's body by making a log. Pinch a head at one end and a pointy tail at the other.

4. Gently press the shell onto the body.

5. Give your snail feelers with an eye at each end.

Easy Inchworm

1. Roll lots of little green balls. Make them all about the same size.

2. Gently press the little balls together in a line.

3. Add eyes. Then bend your inchworm to help it inch along!

Fluttering Butterfly

1. Partly mix together two or more colors of Model Magic® Then make two large balls and two small ones.

2. Press the balls together and flatten them as you see here.

3. Roll a rope of another color for your butterfly's body. Press it between the wings. Then add short strings for feelers.

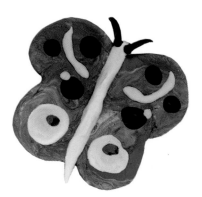

4. Decorate your butterfly's wings! Press on dots and strings of Model Magic® to make pretty designs.

Pond, Sweet Pond!

Snappy Turtle and Friendly Froggy live in a pond. Other animals live there, too!

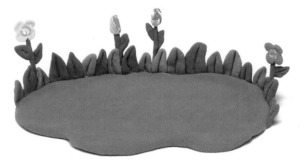

1. Make the pond by flattening a big piece of blue Model Magic.® Make the edges curvy just like a real pond.

2. Put some plants around the pond. Mold stems and leaves with green Model Magic.®

3. Set the turtle on its rock—and the frog and its lily pad, in the pond.

What other pond animals can you add? How about the bugs you made on pages 28–30?

More Fun with Model Magic®!

1. To make something that will stand up tall, mold Model Magic® around toothpicks, craft sticks, or straws. The stems for these flowers were made by pressing green Model Magic® around toothpicks.

2. Press craft feathers, pipe cleaners, beads, or dried beans into your Model Magic® project before it dries.

ISBN 0-439-33617-1

Designed by Julie Mullarkey   Model Magic® art created by Julie Mullarkey & Deborah Schecter

12 11 10 9 8 7 6 5 4 3   3 4 5 6/0
Printed in the U.S.A.
First Scholastic printing, November 2001

Keep finished product away from open flame. Do not mold into candleholders or other like items for use around flame. Do not put in oven, microwave or kiln.